Poetry for Now
*A Collection of Verse from
the Heart of Modern Britain*

A De Sales Book

Published 2012 by arima publishing

www.arimapublishing.com

ISBN 978 1 84549 566 4
© First De Sales Limited Partnership, 2012

Printed and bound in the United Kingdom

arima publishing
ASK House, Northgate Avenue
Bury St Edmunds, Suffolk IP32 6BB
t: (+44) 01284 700321

www.arimapublishing.com

Poetry for Now
A Collection of Verse from the Heart of Modern Britain

Contents

Introduction

Poetry for Now is an anthology of remarkable modern poems from Britain's corporate community. This is a sector whose creative talent has all too often been overlooked or ignored which means that little, if any, corporate poetry exists in print. *Poetry for Now* addresses this imbalance by presenting a collection of over eighty previously unpublished poems that have been authored by a diverse range of professionals including surgeons, company CEOs, accountants and City financiers, from every corner of this Sceptred Isle and across every age group.

The origins of the *Poetry for Now* project lie within the First De Sales Limited Partnership, a creative writing partnership that brought together individuals from across the United Kingdom. De Sales has tried to redress an acknowledged lack of published corporate poetry by asking those involved to write their own works. When it came to style and length, contributors were given a free hand: the only stipulation was that a poem's central theme should concern something 'modern', although how this should be interpreted was left up to the individual.

The result is a collection of original, high quality poems which utilise a diverse range of themes, styles and topics. Some of the poems are light-hearted and humorous while others deal with some of the toughest problems that currently face British society, the environment and even the world. Although the poets were given a free hand, their results have been grouped into eight chapters, each based around a loose theme.

Poetry for Now is a simple but unorthodox idea whose high-quality verse will provoke emotional thought and debate amongst those that read it. Judging by the results of this volume, the new field of corporate poetry is set to become an established part of the wider creative writing genre.

Humour

Online Sonnet

Shall I Facebook poke thee on a summer's day?
Your profile picture's beauty hath no end.
My tweets reveal what my heart hath to say:
On Myspace I request *you* to be my friend.
Blogging may not romantic seem to thee,
But your Youtube videos make my heart race,
I hope this SMS will make you see,
Nothing says love like a smiley face.
On webcam you look so bright, your eyes do shine
'Til I realise it's just the settings on Skype,
I email you compliments to make thee mine,
And try to woo you with the words I type.
I LOL with happiness because it won't be long,
'Til you and I find each other on match.com.

Archaeology

Do you agree, or is it me?
I'm foxed by archaeology.

You dig up stuff that's ancient,
A thousand years or more,
You label it and box it up,
Then lock it in a store.

No one gets to see them.
One thousand boxes full
Of a million Roman artefacts
Wrapped in cotton wool.

All numbered, labelled, put away
Saved for another day.
They once were 'lost' but at least that way
I could have found one for myself some day

Let's not bother digging.
They need never to be found.
Just leave them where they are,
Safely underground.

Financial Mnemonics

The world of finance is complex and strange
With ISA's and gilts, and rates of exchange.
EISs and bonds, and VCTs,
PINCs and tax, and PPPs.
All designed to confuse the common man
Because perplexity means the Government can
(Along with bankers and umpteen FAs)
Create a convoluted maze,
Of terms and obscure financial mnemonics
All dressed up as sound economics

To help the punter for the future save
To avoid becoming serf or slave;
Take his money with permission
Don't explain in full, commission,
Hidden charges, or costs up front,
But, by pulling the wizardly stunt,
Of sounding off in terms highbrow
The benefits of investing now
To create a healthy future sound
Where increased capital will abound

And "by placing funds with me,
We'll help you cut your IHT."
So reassured, with your money you'll part
Knowing he has your interests at heart;
And any future diminutions
Of your hard earned contributions
Is down to exceptional market forces,
Unforeseen drops in the world's resources
Or bankers gambling with your money,
Creating pots of honey
From which bonuses can be paid
Without responsibility laid
On their shoulders, or their actions;
"It is down to other factions!"
The moral? Let it clearly be said:
Keep your money under your bed.

Soliloquy

By way of aside to this soliloquy,
This meaningless monologue, all about me,
Of which it's been said, quite wrongfully
That the author's subsumed, so completely
That whenever he writes his mindless scree
All that's achieved is crass whimsy.
I wanted to say something quite worthy
About how I used to be so carefree
That my days would be spent in the shade of a tree,
Writing and waxing lyrically,
Not rushing or acting too hastily
Nor creating a piece that is too wordy
But taking my time, working slowly,
Showing respect and subtlety,
Embracing my topic entirely
And crafting my piece accordingly,
Using my metaphors sparingly
Comparing my verse to the crash of the sea
And then, very occasionally,
Switching to bring in a simile
As big as a house; or as small as a bee

That's when I felt strongest, creatively
But now that I'm old and all too weary
My writing and waxing is waning, you see
And gone is the witty repartee.
All that is left is something vaguely
Sad, frustrated and all too lonely;
A shadow of how I used to be.
So when people ask if this piece was me,
I can hold up my head and say happily
That indeed it was I who upped the ante
With a poem that rhymed from beginning to end.

Haute Cuisine

Kaleidoscopic colours and shapes
In homage to van Gogh or Renoir,
Formed and presented by Cartier or Fabergé;
Rare, eclectic ingredients hubbled and bubbled by a
mysterious Merlin.

Textures and sounds of sensual, alluring femmes fatales,
Soft moans of ecstasy as the lips and tongue are caressed;
Taste buds wallow in a cascade of flavours;
Aromas worthy of Guerlain,
And yet, the one inescapable bouquet,
Is of fifty pound notes, smouldering away.

Going Green

I wish I were a tree-hugger,
A green and worthy man,
Supporting Greenpeace and environmentalists
In every way I can.

Eating veg and muesli,
Cycling everywhere;
Championing wimmin's rights and the like;
Recycling all that's there.

But then again, I'm having fun
Driving in my car;
Eating meat, and keeping warm
And propping up the bar.

Buy it. Use it. Chuck it out.
'Disposable's the way!'
Couldn't give a toss what others think,
Never mind what they might say.

For I'm a good old-fashioned bloke
Who knows just where it's at;
A misogynistic, unbelieving,
Self-important prat.

Modern Limericks

Take a guy with a ball but no brain
And teach him the beautiful game
With a place in the squad
Make him richer than God
And his ego will grow with each day

I saw a young swan turn to a goose
Her clothes and her tongue rather loose
Selling her soul to the rags
To pay for her fags
Please madam, become a recluse

Quit work for celebrity fame
Simply by playing the game
Get a foot in the door
Be flirtatious and more
Next Botox and silicon gain

It's all I could possibly dream
Quite sad when I'm only fifteen
Please Simon say yes
Or it's a job like the rest
I need to be on the big screen

Haiku

A very short poem
From the Rising Sun
For very short people
Who have no fun.

Collective

I saw a pride of lions chase a fall of lambs
Whilst a family of otters ate an entire bed of clams
Amidst the bellowing of finches and
to the exaltation of the larks
The pitying of the turtledoves took place in several parks
But 'twas the shrewdness of the apes,
that secured the bunch of grapes

The unkindness of the ravens led to the murder of the
crows
But it was the business of the ferrets,
which we all wanted to know
As a scoop of journalists and a clutch of car mechanics
Fought over which of them was more worthy and
almost, in their panic
Fell down a flight of stairs into a conference of pears

I hear a pod of dolphins and a mob of kangaroos
Elected a coalition of cheetahs to a Parliament of fools
Or a parliament of owls as wise as owls can be
May yet create a richness of pine martens,
we will have to wait and see
More likely another crash of rhinoceroses
and then a skulk of foxes

There stood a brace of dentists in the pouring rain
Waiting at the station for a cancellation of trains
"We need a virtue of patients", one of the dentists cried
"Not just a quango full of wasters, then?"
the other one replied
I don't know but I've a hunch,
the collective noun for bankers is a wunch!?

Economy

Fallen Covers

Dusty shelves.
Sealed letter-box.
No sign of the life which once was:
Empty window displays;
Quiet despair;
The shop remembers old days.

When laughing children rushed in after school,
For the daily story telling of a new book.
When Christmas shoppers flooded in after work,
Buying thoughtful treats for their loved ones.
When lonely old ladies popped inside to ask,
If the new knitting manual had arrived yet.

Dusty shelves.
Forgotten promises.
Drained completely of all its life.
Cardboard boxes
Containing tattered remains;
The shop ponders what could have been.

New books were launched with exciting offers;
Buy three for two, or two for one.
Shelves groaned under the weight of best-sellers,
Literary works of art, swapping words for paint.
The bell above the shop door tinkled constantly
As each shopper entered the magical world of books.

Dusty shelves.
Abandoned cash-till.
The shop mourns its own death.
Unloved and unwanted,
What the internet had started,
The recession finished off.

The Recession

The recession.
Unemployment and depression.
People have no money but, for the rich, it's an obsession.
For the rich money's but an object: that's the impression.
Rumours that the recession is over and finished,
Yet families live like residents of a third world village.

The rich still have money to blow,
While villagers have no water to flow.
Money makes the world go round,
The recession's made the economy go down,
It had a fall with no autumn but, whatever the season,
Love should revolve the world;
Money shouldn't be the reason.

Asset Bubbles

The oil that feeds consumption is running out of breath.
Sovereign States are quantitatively easing to near death.
The asset bubbles fuelled by credit were doomed to die.
Securitising the world added up to one big lie.

Do investment bankers or hedge funds really care?
They'll continue to profit off the backs of the damned,
Who die of starvation in far off lands.
So we're no further forward, just further along,
Using PR consultants to defend what is wrong.

If an eye for an eye remains the rule,
We're going to end up in a room of blind fools.
We're asleep in our financially engineered hell,
And regulation will not protect us from death's knell.

But the few can only trample down the many for so long,
History teaches us the consequences of wrong.
Our souls are asleep; it's time to wake up. It's not too late.
Before our children suffer our own fate.

Letter, not Spirit

How many acronyms do you know?
Finance gives you plenty. Try CDO.
Collateralized Debt Obligation,
Technical wizardry. Innovation.
Gather lots of different debts, mix them in a pile,
It can't go wrong; you have to smile.
Subprime. Auto loans; throw them all in,
With the yields they're paying, you're bound to win.
Figure out the rules the agencies use,
Cut the pile to fit, you really can't lose.
Get some weak debt that might not be repaid,
Mix in some good stuff: the foundations are laid.
Decide who loses first when someone can't pay,
But they'll get the highest coupon;
Cross your fingers and pray.
The slice from the top is solid: triple A,
At least if the world works like the agencies say.
As safe as the debt of the strongest state,
But how do we do it? Paying a much higher rate.
Something for nothing? Surely not? No?
Grab a hard hat when the world starts to blow.

So how is this magic wrought?

A very simple predication:
In the worst of times defaults have imperfect correlation.
Bad times for one does not mean trouble for another,
So with your mixture, you'll always have some cover.
Historical simulation told ratings agencies this was true,
The problem with history is that each day it is something new.

A few lonely voices doubt the value of debt,
Wager on a fall in the price: looks like a good bet.
The voices become less lonely and the chorus rises higher,
A screaming, piercing chant of "Fire! Fire! Fire!"
Panic in the market is like panic of any sort,
In the rush for safety, people are caught.
Blind to value, blind to what went before,
The one thing that matters is getting out of the door.
The magic is broken. All debts seem as one.
That simple predication, unravels. It comes undone.

Investors lose money, crushed in a stampede,
But what of the banks that encouraged their greed?
The worst of the mix, at the base of the pile,
Selling that on to customers often took style.

At the height of the panic it all turned to dust,
When the banks readied themselves to go bust.
Millions and billions of dollars; where did it go wrong?
Believing that alphabet letters made investments look
strong.
But triple A counts for nothing when it's the output rules
Of an imperfect model that misunderstands its fools.
The rules were bent and dressed up mutton as lamb,
Sticking to the letters but, in spirit, just a sham.

21st Century Pillage

Greed, greed, let's grow some more.
We can own everything we like.
The stupid investors will finance it all
While we make more and have a ball.

That it isn't our money need not be a worry,
Rather, let's own it, and take the carry.
The shareholders they want it:
Do they know what they're getting?
I guess not, given all of their fretting.

A one-sided bet.
Get it right and take all of the spoils.
Get it wrong and the politicians bail them out,
'Cos they know their bankers always look after them.

Thank the generous fellow who pays,
By giving him less interest on his hard earned cash,
By charging him more (if we lend to him at all),
Well, how else can we afford to have a ball?

Work

The Conference Call

We sat around the table
While the grey plastic starfish
Grimly proclaimed its analysis in a foreign monotone:
'From these figures we can predict
Much lower profitability across
Almost all of our product lines, right?'

No one listened. No one heard.
Neither Josh in khakis; nor Antanas in his suit,
Which was crumbed and crumpled, and flecked with
soup.
With their regulation hair and oyster eyes,
Their features were dead, anesthetized.

And Maria, who was dressed in executive grey,
And had hopes higher than this,
And is unlikely to stay;
She smoothed her hands over skin-tone tights
And combed her fingers through faded highlights.

No one, then, said a word.
And there was nothing to tell.
We dazed, brought on by lunch, the office temperature,
And the inertia of Excel.

The voice continued disjointedly.

'Even discounting the cost initiatives,
And I think it's right to discount them, right?
We can see how we're still going to miss margins and
Be crucified by senior management.'

Fifty-three minutes of this, and not a single second of life.
Just that brittle little voice, stabbing at me like a knife.
Right.

Trading Floor Battleground

They stride in, ready to face the enemy in war.
Day after day, strife and deception are encountered and
defeated.
Is the enemy's enemy my ally?
In the fog sometimes we see more,
But knowledge is the only friend when opponents meet.

This war is an odyssey where we are tied up
Then pulled by lust towards rash decisions.
We drop back to reality as those round us fade into the
past,
their lives hacked short by poor conclusions.
They find themselves making their way down to Hades.

We see ourselves, facing outwards uncertainly
Not knowing which way to face or jump, nerves jangling.
The blood pressure rises, bodies get hot,
The rustle of panic and fear spreads around the field.

The novices lose their calm, panic seizes them.
'Keep still and focus,' mutter the experienced hands,
But they too feel fear seeping into their bones.
They know too well how quickly they could
join their ex-comrades,
Whose names are muttered randomly, darkly, or with
tinges of regret.
The appointed hour passes, and before the information is
even heard,
The rapid increase in activity tells us all we need.
Noise rises across the arena;
The din of hard muster mixes with fear and excitement.

War is joined, and we dive headlong into the fog.
How can we best manage this situation?
First one way, then the other;
We can make no headway and give grudgingly previously
won profit.

It's only one wrong move or unforeseen foe,
That comes at you, with no time to react.
Next to me I see a rash step taken and
The axe comes before you hear it, turning to dust,
Another joins the ghosts of the battlefield.

It feels as if fate is against us but we must make it to
sunset,
For fighting another day is what counts now.
Unknown things overtake us,
And we see others making irrational decisions.

From behind my ear, I hear:
'Hold steady now, we can do this.'
And I steel myself.
Breathing deeply, I lunge,
Execute and step back quickly to examine the carnage.

We have made it, I look around at the battlefield.
Some are near sobbing, others still in the heat of combat.
Done for the day, we retreat warily,
Eyes and ears tuned for any change in strategy needed.

Transport

There once was an airline called CheapyJet
Whose prices were as low as they get,
No leg room at all,
It's hardly a ball,
Not being able to move a safe bet.

Instead there's the tube in the city,
It's so busy, it's rather a pity,
Commuters galore
It's rather a bore
The adverts in it are far from witty.

The trains are late, the buses are slow,
Public transport can be such a blow,
Parking's a nightmare
I don't even care
Walking's the only way to go.

Work, Work, Work...

Do we work to live?
Or do we live to work?

We work to live and live to die;
We work so hard but just to get by.

We live like this every day;
There's not enough time to stop and play.

The world flies by so fast,
Before you know the time has passed.

We only stop at the end;
Our bodies age and never mend.

We work ourselves to the ground,
Until we lie beneath a mound.

Dead to the world, we're soon forgotten.
Under the ground, we'll soon be rotten.

Consider this and stop to think;
It could be gone before you blink.

Retirement

Dear John,

A man, age sixty; been around for a while.

Known for his capabilities, his wit and his smile.

It is time to sit back; rest on your laurels for a while.

Take Janis out,

Hold hands. Treat her in style.

Blessed with a family and lots of good friends,

Dear John: Happy sixtieth.

This message I send.

The Interview

The manager loosened his tie and licked his lips
And, leaning towards her, placed his fingertips
On the table gently.
His eyes dripped closed.
For a moment, nothing was said.
Presently, he raised a single digit from the vinyl finish
Like a prestigious medium, in communion with the dead.

'The company,' he began. 'The company is growing.'

Glossily, as in a brochure, he eulogised the firm,
Conjuring up its history, speaking of it in terms
So grand that later - much later - alone at night in bed
She would wonder just what it was that day,
That he had said.

'The job itself, of course, has many benefits.'

He polished up the role for her, spat on it and buffed it
bright
And, with a little flourish,
Placed it in the space between them like a rare light of
beauty,
A wish she never knew she had.

From outside, the sounds of the office gathered in
confusion
Drew in around them like nightfall in winter,
Like the shortening days.
She felt snug there.

He snapped his fingers. She opened her eyes.
He quizzed her briefly on the VAT rise,
And made a few surprising comments about his own
health,
His passion for sea fishing
And of opportunities for the creation of wealth.
Then it was finished.

She left breathless and uneasy, and with a sense
That what had passed between them in that room
Had somehow diminished them both: her and him.

The Office Blaggard

The office blaggard is a joy to behold.
As he swaggers, and tells of his stories so bold.
His conquests, thrice nightly, explicit he boasts.
(Though we know that his bedsheet his seed has seen most.)

Of racecars and airplanes, upon all he has rode.
And thus he fancies himself some master of those.
Yet when challenged for details, enquiries by peers.
Away from the throng, to toilet disappears.

He does not want the poor masses to find,
That his life no more interesting than yours, or mine.

So when the time comes.
That a story he runs.
Allow him his time.
For in his head, he does shine.

Am I a Yummy Mummy?

I start my day,
Tired.
I shower, shave, moisturise and blow dry my hair.
I carefully apply natural make up.
My clothing is the perfect balance of sexy and strong,
Yet demure.
When I see my people,
I smile.
I am confident.
Although, I am aware;
That I like to be thought of as being more intelligent,
More wealthy,
More beautiful than I fear I really am.
I am often surrounded by childish antics and tantrums.
My day is long.
Is it productive?
Have I made a difference?
Maybe I have.
Maybe, today I helped mould,
Helped influenced,
The next Obama?
But I am not a Yummy Mummy.
I am a Banker.
A Banktress.

London Poem

Oh London, London, why did I leave?
Why did I desert you? What did I perceive?
The place I loved and lived for 15 years, the place to be,
A centre of mixed culture and global urbanity,
I loved the buzz, I loved the hive,
The great city which seemed always alive.
I admired the museums and Regents Park,
I cherished the busy theatre life in the dark.
I loved the restaurants and pubs and Claridge's afternoon
tea,
The new places to be found, round the corner to see.

Beside all this beauty, all the joyful rides,
The city developed other less pleasant sides.
I thought I had this London energy forever that I could
burn
But after years of happiness, my life took a turn.

The everyday commute became a jiggle,
It got worse each year,
Too crowded. No space, just sweat, too late, too slow,
The tube began to make my nerves wriggle

It became more of a strain, waiting for the train,
The display showing two minutes wait.
Two minutes that became stretched and late;
The two turned to five; and five went to ten,
Still two minutes are shown,
The platform overcrowded; they start closing it down.

A train arrives, no space for me,
Or no-one else in the waiting platform community.
Another five trains pass; another 30 minutes down the line,
Finally inside the train,
People shoving and poking their elbows at mine.
With the next breath just a finger-thick away from me,
I start asking myself: Is this the place I want to be?

The car's not an option.
The street's clogged and with cars overgrown,
The constant traffic jam and stop and go
Would fire my heart rate up high and turn my mood low.

Looking at real estate: another sad joke,
The price of houses made me broke.
Those millions of pounds for a home to be,
But at the end, too many flaws appear and scream at me.
With the contract exchanged and monies all paid,
No return out of the house, it's too late,
The wind blowing through the bricks,
The lights breaking down,
The heating works neither, it makes me frown;
The doors won't shut properly, the boiler is old,
The water pressure seems more weaker than bold.
With all these things burning me out and facing me,
I keep asking myself: Is this the place I still want to be?

Then I considered with my head low,
What does my life consist of now?
Working 14 hours like a horse on a track,
With the never-ending pressure and sweat
Always close to a heart attack.
The constant delays on the way to work and back
A clogged up nose and a hurtful neck,
My day-to-day life was off the track,
And the final straw at the end
Was Mr Darling raising taxes to 50 percent.

After full-thinking, I figured out,

It's a new city I need to think about.

Oh London, oh London, I just had to go; to find a new kind,

I just had to leave you, I hope you don't mind.

You still have a place in my heart and I hope to be

One day right back in your reality.

I hope it will change for the good and the glee,

To feel re-inspired by your global integrity.

Zero Bound

In two thousand and seven, our economy peaked;
First it slowed down, and then it turned weak.
By two thousand and eight we had a recession,
In the fall of that year, there were fears of depression.

The financial authorities, they cut interest rates,
And banks, they were bailed out, not left to their fate.
When rates got to zero, they kept printing cash,
Injecting it all, to prevent a worse crash.

Now time has gone by, the recovery's flat,
Unemployment is high, bond yields pinned to the mat.
There is plenty of slack, and wage growth is slow,
And except for commodities, inflation is low.

Now that assets aren't worth what they once were before,
Defaults have gone up, interest rates stuck on the floor.
But these near-zero rates apply to the most
Credit-worthy of borrowers, the rest they are toast.

The marginal borrower remains quite distressed:
Negative equity, job loss, high rates, and the rest.
So most debtors pay interest above posted rates,
And since they cannot refinance, default them awaits.

That's how Japan got into its earlier mess,
Although corporates, not households, were their main
source of stress.
Two decades have gone by, and prices are lower,
Than they were twenty years back - and GDP it's gone
nowhere.

It now seems the west will suffer this fate,
Since the measures we've taken are too little, too late.
One way or another, debt burdens will fall,
Through growth, inflation, forgiveness, default.

Now Japan chose the fourth of these routes,
And so far, the west, is following suit.
The Fed's modest attempt to pursue further QEs
Has triggered protest at home and overseas.

The least path of resistance is default and deflate,
Which is painful for all and is such a waste
Of resources that could, be producing today,
But when public opinion's opposed, there's no way.

The Good Life

For nigh on fifty years
You've worked for the same company
But then, when you reach sixty-five
It's time for you to leave
You set off for the office
On your final day
A golden handshake and a carriage clock
Then they send you on your way

This is the Good Life that you always talked about
A healthy pension, is that all?
Welcome to the Good Life, a lovely country home
With ivy growing up the wall

Will they all remember you?
In the years to come
Will they speak of "Good old George"
And all the things you've done
Or will you be forgotten
And your name rubbed from the file
I guess they will be talking about you
But only for a very short while

This is the Good Life, retirement at its best
A chance to take it easy for a bit
Hello to the Good Life, the tranquillity of it all
A place where no one gives a shit

You always did love toiling
In the garden all day
Now it's the only thing you have left
To pass the time away
The carriage clock above the fire
Chimes time for tea
Buttered scones and strawberry jam
Have become so routine

This is the Good Life they told you to enjoy
So spend your time in your own way
An Englishman's home is his castle
Where family never comes to stay

You miss the stress
Of an active brain
You can't stop fussing around
Endlessly worrying
You wish you were still at work
Though you felt like a slave
But this life of rest
Is driving you to an early grave

This is the Good Life where people come to die
We'll sit and watch them as they fall
A country graveyard, with roses in the front
And ivy growing up the wall

Business IQ (Haiku)

BEGINNINGS
An idea evolves
Sweaty equity required
Creation of life

THE PEOPLE
Your team are first class
Driving business forward
Look after them well!

TEMPUS FUGIT
Manage your time well
Control those distractions or -
They will control you

STRESS BUSTERS UNITE
Why are we upset?
At inanimate objects
Such as computers

THE ANSWER
Not about money
Activity generates -
Business success

THE PROBLEM
Is not the problem
It's your reaction that counts
Perception is all

GIVE ME SNAIL MAIL
Email is so fast
A letter tells the story
So much more fully

THE END IN MIND
Planned independence
Removes unplanned dependence
Success is assured

CUSTOMERS
They are always right
Awesome service delivers
So listen and learn

Politics

The 2010 General Election

The 2010 general election;
Each party tried to find perfection,
Whilst for us it was a hard selection.
One box ticked could change everything with no scope
for correction.
So what colour did you choose?
Whom did you want to lose?
Each party had so much to prove,
To change the UK, to make it improve.
Cameron got an egg, thrown direct at his head,
Brown called out 'bigot', almost making his campaign
dead.
Labour's chances hung by a thread,
But instead,
We got a mixture of Conservative and the Lib Dem,
So let's see if they can solve any problem,
It's funny how they all tried to stay composed and
intelligent,
Yet five years later it will be a new bunch of lies to stay
relevant.

Faux Pas

Opinionated voter, have your say;
Black and white or shades of grey
'Give me your views,' he wants to hear,
He will listen and appear sincere,
But in the safety of his car,
He will make a small faux pas,
"That bigoted woman," he truly thought
It's all on tape and he's been caught

The Glorious Sixth

It seems a lifetime I've been waiting in these queues,
I've watched the figures multiplying in the News,
Another ship goes down, another drowning crew
But don't complain
Soon, once again
We'll have a chance to choose.

A year for dope and three for coke, as people ease their pain
He got let off, scot-free for 'she was equally to blame',
Out of touch and out of step so far they're almost lame
But soon we choose
And soon we'll lose
Then we can all complain

My heart is strong, I will live long - I am the Nation's health
My soul is weak, I cannot speak so highly for the Nation's wealth
Our taxes and our waistlines grow each day by stealth
But do not fret
Just place your bet
And play the hand you're dealt

Around the world it's true: Religion's still the biggest killer
A bomb, a plane, let's go again, we will emerge the winner
Keep family near and live in fear
And let them wage our war on terror
Choose only one
And bring your gun
Then breathe in deep the horror

Let's teach our children – after me, say A B C D HIV
With people dying as they reach the point of ecstasy
So far from home, they're mostly not at all like you and
me
So let us sweep
And let us keep
Our heart and conscience free

Where are the dreams?
All dead it seems now we have lost our way
It's been so long but nothing's changed, since the sixth of
May
Have no doubt, the truth will out, when each of can say
A yellowish blue
With a greenish hue
I didn't vote for you, no way!?

Democracy Is Coming – the Last Stop

So this is the last stop...
A coalition government has been formed.
We are standing at the gates of a new dawn.
You compromised your principles to gain power.
Found a new form of political partnership to suit the
hour.
Made ministerial salary cuts, to optically improve your
looks.

You've crawled into the gutter to reach so high.
Asked the press officer for another lie.
There's a lot of water under your bridge: lot of other stuff
too.
But don't worry about the truth, its only passing through.

Must be time to find peace with your friends.
Pretend to make amends.
Do you see the fires that burn in the East?
And the hate that runs so deep?

Better teach the country austerity.
Make a virtue out of misery.
Transfer the nation's debt from the greedy to the needy.
Give your friends a helping hand.
Democracy in action in our green and pleasant land.

God's Work

God's work must be hard to do where the son's light is
obscured from view.

Do you wait for the wise men's gifts,

Or do you watch whilst financial markets give profits
another lift?

Do your prophesises preach to the needy,

Or do you prefer to help the greedy?

Are you plagued with self-doubt,

Or is Revelations just too far out?

Are the SEC and Senate Committee the extent of your
morality,

Or do you prefer political and moral neutrality?

Do the poor have a voice,

The jobless, the homeless, a choice?

Or is it all too late,

Has the Maker already opened the gate?

This is no Country for Old Men

Milton you should be living at this hour.
Unhappy breed of men,
Touched by infection and the hand of war,
Stone-faced and set in a tarnished sea.

Here there is no countenance divine,
No arrows of desire,
But blunted flesh in toxic penetration,
Satanic mills lie still.
The work done.
No funds to build Jerusalem
In this green and unpleasant land

It is calm tonight.
But listen,
To the grating roar, begin and cease
And then begin again
On a darkling plain swept with confusion,
Struggle, flight,
As armies of the ignorant clash by night.

No longer the envy of less happy lands
No longer blessed.
This little world,
This sceptic isle,
This travesty of earth,
This piss pot,
This England.

Ad Hoc

Makeshift, gimcrack, what a mess.
Withdraw, retreat and reassess,
'Impossible!' The plan's in place,
'Forward, press on!' to save some face.
Blairite: inept strategy;
Bloody, fatal, tragedy.

Memories of the Noughties

The Millennium Dome,
New Labour on throne.
Dot coms in trouble,
Tweets and pokes the new bubble.

9/11 attack,
7/7 they're back.
An Iraqi quagmire,
IRA ceasefire.

Katrina and Rita show tooth,
An Inconvenient Truth?
Britney and Becks non-stop,
Goodbye to the King of Pop.

iPod unveiled,
iPhone all hailed.
No more free lunch,
All change for the Credit Crunch.

The 2010 Coalition

At first there was the Tories who made promises,
Then next came the Lib Dems who made their own
promises,
Then came the election where voters get to decide who
will break less of the promises made.

At 7am on May 6th the Great British public cast their
votes,
The voters forgot about the old dour Brown and instead
went for a peaceful regime change,
The voters may have been happy but the voters forgot to
give a resounding victory to one of the others.

At once the political fighting began,
Then the agreement between two unlikely bed fellows
started to take form,
Then at last a Coalition was formed – hail the new era was
what was said.

At first blush the Coalition looked great,
The parties however had both agreed what promises to
break,
The parties now had the perfect excuse as it was the
voters' to blame.

At first it was fees for education,
Then it became a question of taxation,
Then the voters really realised their mistake, albeit it was
far too late.

Politicians

To the little politician man whom wishes to shake my hand or hold a baby close for the photo ops that mean the most.

All the promises that I hear get very tired upon my 40 year old ears.

Are you middle, left or right? I know not as you shift your position like the wind to leave my 40 year old mind in riddles.

You shout out promises you cannot keep and I wish you, for 40 years, just fell asleep.

I know that at the end of your day you care not one jot for what I have to say.

To the little politician man whom wishes me to believe, please just go and do something real that I can believe.

The Royal Wedding

A joyful buzz went around the country
As if it was one of our own who was to marry
Clarence House confirmed - another Royal wedding
A fairytale romance (or just an excuse
For a day off work and plenty of booze)
The motherless Prince engenders our pity
And Kate Middleton, a girl so pretty
And smart and gracious
We curiously watch through the media's large window
A moment of hope in our cold thankless winter
The future King? Our future Queen?
What will it all mean?
An ordinary girl – a story with hope
That good will happen to us
And dreams can be realised
We will celebrate, as a nation
As Westminster Abbey lends itself again
To another Royal Wedding

Obama

In 2008, Obama won with much to do;
There was an airy feeling of what he could do.

In 2009, the feeling had taken a dive;
There were so many people he had to keep alive.

In 2010, he passed free health care for all;
But by then he had taken a near fatal fall.

In 2012, Obama faced his second election;
Borrowing all that money from China did not harm his
re-election.

The War on Terrorism

War, the greatest plague of man,
And one's being fought in Afghanistan.
The teens are fighting but don't understand,
Why aren't our differences settled man to man?
It's a war on terrorism,
Which results in stereotypes and racism,
But if you think we should be there, if it's what you
believe,
Then in the end what will we achieve?
Pain and heartache, and a lot of drama,
Which country's next? Cameron's or Obama's?
Imagine this day if you were a soldier,
On a battlefield, keeping composure;
Knowing that today your life could be over.
When you feel down think about what life's like being a
British soldier.

Goodbye to the Gun

My father gave you to his son,
I picked it up when I was young,
Then I believed there was work to be done,
Hello to the gun.

I plotted, we worked,
Other men's demise.
I could not see through others' eyes,
Oblivious to another's cries
My gun and I,
My gun and I.

Now I think about what were achieved,
More death, more hate more pain revealed,
More pain wrecked people,
Eyes cried dry,
There lies our victory you and I,
Time has passed, the blood-stained rivers run
We can't undo what we have done.
And I won't bequeath you
To my son,
Goodbye to the gun,
Goodbye to the gun.

Valediction

Our visitors are leaving my hills and glens,
Leaving my ancient land,
Scarred with the wounds of war,
How can healing be achieved
With bandages of wire?

Soon the blade-chopped, ravaged air
Will return to rest,
When gone forever foreign forts,
From my mother country's chest.

Health

The Death Sentence
Part One: Him

I find it hiding deep within him:

The death sentence.

The enquiring camera lights explain the symptoms, it's clear.

There is a palpable change in the room,

An awkward hush; his life darkly transformed.

A short time of blissful ignorance remains;

He sleeps now, untroubled.

Already half the man and declining, his body will take him in the end.

In a small room he won't remember, his future is delivered

All smiles and optimism taken away in a few short words

The fearful, breathy, brave questions that follow,

The regret, the tests and signs ignored, now too late,

Telling them all is a fearful weight on his chest, dreading the front door closing behind him.

The Death Sentence
Part Two: Me

I see it hiding deep within him; I've learned to find it

A nod and sigh from a nurse, reading the news in my eyes

My well-worn script waits on my tongue as I dread his wakening,

And how I have to end his life with words.

Fear in his drowsy eyes meet mine, wider than normal, hopeful, lying.

The heavy recital is met with a wry nod.

After, we feign cheer and I am bright for his sake

My chest heaves; grateful he made it easy for me, relieved.

When the door closes I begin again, swallowing the knot from my throat.

Remembering the sad sentence I delivered all through my drive home,

Forgetting him as my front door closes, my family waiting for me and smiling.

National Health Service: N-H-S

Nation Health Service: N-H-S.
People on waiting lists: so much stress.
Anticipating but fed up and depressed;
But the NHS takes no interest.
OK, I'm sure some practices are incredible,
And in some hospitals, the meals are edible,
I'm positive that some doctors are highly credible,
But the rules on some matters should be unequivocal.
Appointments aren't meant to be purposely late,
And at least we have a service we can appreciate,
So let me reiterate,
We have the NHS… Let's celebrate.

The NHS: Fact or Fiction?

The NHS: fact or fiction?
You must go further than the diction:
Who's in charge? Who can tell?
It's mostly management numbers that swell.

SHA, PCT, it's all gobbledygook, you see.
Perhaps you can explain the following to me?
Why a London formula must in Yorkshire work?
Doncaster's not Hamstead: tykes don't equate to Berks.

Five years of development funding gone,
That's what Darsi means to me.
Scunthorpe didn't need one, but we had to: you see?
We could have used it better, we say with conviction;
We need hard facts in the NHS and fewer acts of fiction.

Through all the swirling mists of confusion,
A demotivated workforce mired up in the collusion.
This great institution can be made to succeed:
What's fiction? What's fact? What do we need?

The Surgery

The day hits at seven, but I try to postpone,
Just a few precious hours since last fielding the 'phone.
Meet in the morning, computer switched on,
Emails to answer, results to act on.
When surgery starts, it's non-stop for three hours,
Then 'phone calls and messages, letters and forms.

Home visits vary, but always a few,
The young and the elderly, friends old and new.
Back to the surgery, consulting again,
Both parents with children once Dad is at home.
Need to keep records but also with care,
So typing discreetly, remaining aware.

At all times of day, the anxious are there,
The needy, the lonely, those ready to swear
If their needs are not met or perception of such
And sadly reception is where they sound off.
So care of our staff is an integral part
Of our daily routine of pastoral support.

At close of day, when patients are seen,
More urgent paperwork waiting again,
Computer entries checked for completeness,
Colleagues consulted on delicate issues.
All the time conscious of confidentiality,
Respect for our patients, our staff and each other.

Back-up of data at 10pm,
So all must be looked at and entered by then,
Then to home and all that waits there,
Grateful to go to my bed when spared.
Twice-monthly evening hospital meetings,
Useful, instructive, stimulating, tiring.

Why do I stay when already past sixty?
Why not bow out and enjoy so much else?
The trust and hopes of those seeking help
The on-going needs, the friendship they bring,
The privilege conferred by their faith in me,
The love and support of colleagues and friends.

The Shelf

Is it worth the effort I ask myself?
I'll get another pill down from the shelf
Looking at the bottle thinking of the past
Will I ever get better? Will I last?
I'll keep on trying; I'll get there in the end
Will you be beside me and be my friend
I need someone to help me on my journey
Yes is all you need to say
Just be beside me on the sad days
So they don't turn into really bad days
Is it worth the effort I ask myself?
As I get another pill down from the shelf.

An Unknown Plight

To float through the deathly darkness,
As ghosts and ghouls envelop past,
Bloodstained memories wishing to
Be forgotten in the mist,
Suspended in the still of the night,
Neglected tombstones, diseased, to crumble
Into the elements far beneath,
Whispering branches, secrets shared,
Haunting winds of long-lost lives,
Travel through their endless journey,
Death is not the end but an unknown plight,
To creep along its desperate way
For the new life enters the modern world.

The Worried Well

As I sat eating breakfast
One cold wet winters' day,
A plate of eggs and bacon
And toast upon my tray,
A letter from my surgery
Inviting me to see
A practice nurse to carry out
A health check – just for me.

I haven't seen a doc for years,
I thought with rising fear.
What if they find I'm going to die?
Will they tell me loud and clear?
I'll read *The Guardian*'s women's page
To see what I might get,
And go prepared with lists of facts
Printed from my internet.

And so it was that all that week
I read and studied hard,
And wrote down lots of questions
Upon a piece of card,
To ask about my prostate
And find out what they think
Of checking serum levels
Of magnesium and zinc.

My appointment came and in I went
To see the HCA,
Who poked and pricked and measured me
In every single way.
"You'd better see a doctor now,"
She said in anxious tones.
"You're fat and lazy and you smoke,
So you won't reach old bones."

He looked at me through half-moon specs –
I knew the news was bad.
"Your CVD risk's high, you know –
But we'll sort you out, my lad.
A pill or two will make you feel
Much better than before,
And, with a bit of luck, you'll find
You live past fifty-four."

"First up, let's talk cholesterol –
You'll need a low fat diet.
And Simvastatin I'll prescribe –
I think you'll need to try it.
It can give you muscle pains
And make you feel depressed,
And rot your liver too, you know –
But well check that with a test."

"If you get low, come back to me
And tell me that you cry,
For I can cure that too, my friend,
With an SSRI.
That may make you sweat and want to eat –
Which brings me to your weight.
Your BMI at thirty-two
Is really far too great."

"For that I'll start you on this pill –
We call it Orlistat.
We only offer them to people
Who are far too fat.
It turns your stools to greasy slime
Which seeps out from your bottom,
So please make sure when going out
Your pad is not forgotten."

"Let's now discuss your high BP –
We call it hypertension.
Untreated you will have a stroke,
I probably should mention.
I'll try an ACE – but just low dose
And monitor urea,
'coz kidney function can decline
And make you feel quite queer"

"And if you cough, an ARB
Could be tried instead.
Or perhaps a beta blocker but
Then you won't perform in bed.
Erectile dysfunction can be cured
With Viagra, I'm sure you know,
But only with a private script
At twenty quid a throw."

"An Aspirin too will lower your risk
Of having an MI,
And if it makes your stomach bleed,
I'll add a PPI.
You may grow breasts with that, in time,
And may get hyponatraemia,
But I'm sure you will agree with me –
That's better than anaemia."

"Your urine is quite clear though,
I'm very pleased to say,
But I'll test for prostate cancer so
I'll do your PSA.
So face the wall and bend your knees
And swallow all your pride,
While I prepare to pop a digit
Into your fat backside."

So now I feel as if I live
Down at my local surgery,
And lead a life no better than
I would imagine purgatory.
A blood test here, a BP there
And clinics to stop smoking
And to manage weight and exercise –
I really am not joking.

So there it is – you should beware
Of health checks that aren't wanted,
Lest you become what I am now –
A soul that's deeply haunted
By the thought of what I cost
And the time I waste as well,
By being a paid up member of
The loathsome worried well.

The Grotesqueness of Me

The advice that you gave me
Came too late to save me
My own worst enemy
Too little, too late
And too thin at the waist
I saw my destiny

Everyone stared at me that night
But no one could see my plight
Why can't they see?
The grotesqueness of me

The problem they said
Is in my head
If it's there at all
They can't hope to see
As they're not me
So I just let it go

A monster that rose from her tomb
The ugliest sight in the room
Still no one can see
The grotesqueness of me

So drawn and so pale
So sallow and frail
The target's unclear
Tortured by doubt
Both inside and out
The end may be near

On this path to perfection I'll stay
Won't let beauty stand in my way
They are starting to see
The grotesqueness of me

Environment

A Life

Thought I saw something move.
A flickering of light.
A rooftop almost out of sight.
The shredded remains of a plastic bag's life
Twist and swirl through the night.

It's not eco-friendly.
Has little to offer.
No airs and graces.
No stories from far off places.

It appears as a bird: a Raven, a Hawk.
Turns to me as if to talk.
Knows the best I'm going offer is a walk.
Says don't worry about that tonight.
Come on now and fly.
Come on now: let's fly...

The Planet

The world is finite; resources are scarce,
Things are bad and will get worse,
Coal is burned and gas exploded,
Forests cut and soil eroded,
Wells run dry and air polluted,
Dust is blowing, trees uprooted,
Oil is going, ores depleted,
Drains receive what is excreted,
Land is sinking, seas are rising,
Man is far too enterprising,
Fires will rage with man to fan it,
Soon we will have a plundered planet.

There is no World but this One

The world has many answers
Some of which never reveal themselves
Without the existence of time
Our Time will cease to exist
When the world can give us no more

Illusion is the creation of man, not nature
Nature is not illusive
Nature is the revelation
Unfortunate it is that we do not fathom this
Too late too late
The bells of extinction can be heard
Yet an echo in the distance
We have entered the tunnel
On a one way track
There is no way back

Could we have wavered off this course
Veering left we were
Veering right we were
We tried
Not hard enough
So many passengers
Interested only in the journey
So many drivers, interested only in profit

There was nature
The lifeblood of the human race
Spilt on the gutters in decay
Little trace remains today

Lessons Learned

When we unveil the foggy mist
Created by modern man
The lush green meadows are revealed
The flow of life is ever present
Songs can be heard
In the heavens above
In the oceans below

All that exists makes mockery of the modern man
Where is our purpose
What was our purpose
We disrupted the flow of life
It was entrusted to us
Guardians we were
Failed we did

Joy and happiness. Pain and suffering.
Twinned aren't they always?
Escape them we cannot
Nature does not allow it
We cannot stop it
All time is finite
All progress is ultimately self-destructive
Harmony was the only way
What a price we had to pay

Need for Climate Controls

Without international travel - and all its carbon emissions - what small life I may have lived.

What a small world I may have seen, if I, like you, had not been so keen.

What about a lot of culture I may have missed.

What a small world I may have seen, if I, like you, had not been so keen.

What about a lot of people and friends I may have missed.

What a small world I may have seen, if I, like you, had not been so keen.

What about a lot of scenic views I may have missed.

What a small world I may have seen, if I, like you, had not been so keen.

What a large world my children may have seen, if I, unlike you, had not been so keen.

Dirty Footprint

The first chill breeze on waning sun, puts nature's house in order.

The swallows, graceful, feathered bones, gather in a chitter of excitement,

Their thank you and farewell, seen by blind eyes and heard by deaf ears as

They struggle to the sun for a warmth that some will never feel.

No wars to fight, no footprint left to soil the earth, a stillness in their wake.

The clattering of the snow geese pricks the gloom of autumn's cloak.

Speared south by cold they scratch man's winter wastelands to survive,

But famine is poor credit to man who seeks his pound of flesh.

They pick no fight, only seek to use the lands passed on to share.

One, no footprint left to soil the earth, the other deep in footprint.

Far north, ice crystal beauty masks the harshness of the earth.

Mighty fur ,trapped by winter, crawls from his cavern in the snows.

A snow bath in the sun and white matted fur is clean once more, but

Warm seas melt his highway of survival, as man's dirty footprint travels far.

He leaves no footprint to soil the earth but others tramp and kill.

Winter also pushes man to warmth but in his pleasure seeking world.

No wings, he travels without stress, spewing fumes high in the sky.

No strife, his appetite knows no bounds, with conscience rarely pricked.

His highway wide and ever stretching, must never meet a challenge.

Ever wars to fight and mouths to feed, his dirty footprint tramples on.

Wooded valleys and mountain slopes stand in man's forward path as

Nature's houses burn. The gusting smoke, parting spirits of the trees.

New residents now but with no shelter or welcome on the doors and

Survival now takes second place as avaricious man tramps on.

His dirty footprint spins round a planet which no longer is his guardian.

This Disposable Society

The world today's so different to the one we knew before
This disposable society is something we deplore.
In each and every walk of life we chuck excess away,
So much waste accumulates in just one single day.

We'll decorate the living room, the hall, the kitchen too.
We'll buy new furniture and drapes and paint of different
hue.
Let's not forget the flooring – we'd better get a skip.
We really don't want this "old" stuff – we'll take it to the
tip.

Washers, fridges, freezers, tellies - cast out just on a whim,
The fashion's changed: white's "old hat", let's buy some new
ones in.
The supermarkets must admit they, too, could take some
blame,
Excess packaging galore. No, life's really not the same.

It's just the same outside the house when sorting out the
garden
And if I do repeat myself I really beg your pardon.
We cut the lawn and lop the trees, we take out weeds
a'plenty.
Where does it go? To the tip, of course, with trips of more
than twenty.

And worst of all, it doesn't stop with materialistic things,
It carries on its dogged path and involves wedding rings.
We seem to think it's quite alright to mess up people's lives.
We give no thought to the emotional stress we put on husbands and wives.

Our children think it's quite ok – when broken get one new.
Toys or bikes, friends or Dads or, sometimes, even Mums too.
What about our feelings? Are they just to be thrown away
Like every sack of garbage we rid ourselves of each day?

Why are we so thoughtless, so selfish, self-indulgent?
Why has persevering become so utterly repugnant?
Whatever happened to working hard and earning every penny
And being satisfied with life and respected by so many?

That is all part of a bygone era we'll never see again.
The respect has gone, communities too and, at times, life seems all in vain.
Neighbourliness, loyalty, integrity, truelove, all these we'll see no more.
Yes, this disposable society is something we really deplore!

The Darkness

The great dark cloud loomed across the hill
The air, sea, trees and sky all became still
It was as if we knew, their world and I
It was all to come, the time to cry
But wait, but wait I want to say
Please don't turn and walk away
The time has come
The deed is done
Has another chance been and gone.

Fields and Cities

This life is a flowing river,
A trickling stream,
Running through valleys,
Fields and cities.

With each turn comes,
Something new,
A fresh start or from something learnt,
A new experience to guide us,
Into the modern changed world.

With every turn we take,
And each move we make,
New opportunities arise,
For us to make the world better.

Hence let's cherish these moments,
As this world is too precious,
And time too short,
For us to miss.

Society

The Youth

The youth: apparently an out of control generation.

Vent up anger full of frustration.

But if we got off their back and gave them ventilation,

Would they think about their actions give it some consideration?

The youth who need inspiration;

The teens that need motivation;

To aspire to be a doctor a president,

Not impressing their peers to remain relevant.

Because everyone is unique and intelligent,

And impacts on the world like a stomp of an elephant.

Not everyone is about gangs, guns and drugs,

Let's not get stereotypical; they all can't be thugs,

So give them space; let them grow,

Because the youth of today are our future tomorrow.

Crime

Corruption and violence,

Another youth dead a moment of silence.

Stop think … Why guns why knives?

Their excuse: 'nothing better to do with our lives.'

For money: it's robbery and burglary,

Or murderers, taking lives purposely.

But lies won't save you from perjury,

Or people beaten battered; rushed to accident and emergency.

Then follows surgery.

Young girls: abused and tortured.

Races: being verbally slaughtered.

And all of this is simply crime, crime, crime.

One word but millions of topics brought to my mind.

Exams

Letters like barbed wire, words like little blue ants
Crawling cross the page, scratching in between the lines
Of paper, lined paper, lines like railway tracks
Which teachers tell me can take me places, pathways to
university
Degrees and office jobs and private pensions…
Meanwhile the clock's hands seem to spin and spin,
As I'm desperately trying to fit the words in,
And the lead in my pencil is wearing thin,
But not half as thin as this idea that they've drilled in
That exams are really that important.

Life

One minute we may
Be secure with a job.
Next employment
The economy may rob.

Life brings many storms,
Often without warning.
Or arrive suddenly
With high winds and flooding.

One minute we are healthy,
The next in the hospital sick.
May have swine flu,
But pray not a dose of arsenic.

We can't control or prevent
The storms in our life
Any more than we can prevent
Times of conflict and of strife.

Rock of Ages

Chronology should not be too tight a fit.
Why not choose an age, if you're happy with it?
Crass public opinion (even friends) can be mean
About all of those years when you stayed seventeen.
But what is a number? A symbol. No more.
Like earrings from Gucci; or a dress from Dior.

So why shouldn't our age be worn like our shoes?
Wear slingbacks, or nineteen, whenever we choose.
In the mornings you try on a confident forty;
But slip on thirty-one when feeling naughty.
In the evening you're out in a short twenty-two.
(It may feel too tight but it looks good on you.)

So many years of itinerant fashions;
So many styles, absurd fads and passions.
Why shouldn't we clothe ourselves in false youth?
Why insist on wearing a straightjacket of truth?
As you wear with the years, choose what you wear;
From the vast range of ages at vanity fair.

This be the Worst

They mess you up, these poorly souls
They may not mean to but they do
They tell you of their ails and woes
And add some extra just for you

But they were schooled in their primacy
By ne'er-do-wells in tracky suits
Who who half the time were out of their tree
And half arguing with men in boots

Man hands on misery to man
It deepens when there is no prospect
Stay away as far as you can
For otherwise you may be next
(Props to Mr larkin)

Old Age Titans

When the titans were forced from grace,
From skylight to skirting board,
Thrust to the depths of the Earth
And beyond by Zeus's almighty arm,
Even the tallest of Titans shrank in stature.
Shrivelled and stale, smelly as an old man,
Sitting like dried up fruit in a bowl of mouldering apples,
Past wizened and instead aged off the tree – not rotting,
Not exactly, no. Sinking and sinking into the back of an
ever-reclined armchair,
Sinking into folds of skin that suck onto cheeks once
strong and full,
A face now slack in meaning.

When the Titans were forced from the sky,
Did Zeus spend time testing various hells-on earth?
No, he merely looked to earth itself, where the elderly
hover
On the edge of life;
The edge of the earth, imprisoned
In bodies slumping into husks
In fusty, dinge-laden lairs of unconsciousness
And glancing insanity, shrieks of envy, and angry,
misplaced sociability,
Attended by the hawkish, the dumpy and the dour.
The false cheer scrawled on whiteboards
Distressingly loveless to their blank gaze.

No, there was no need to ensure the malaise of his
forefathers
When the threads of time are destined to fray
And fritter away, the fundamental evaporation of lucidity
and lustre

Shining silks are tossed out in their turn.
And so are we all.

Task

Once upon a time I was given a task,
Of sorting the office, of this I must ask;
Why me? What crime didst I commit.
What crime that the punishment this must fit.

First I started with papers, this was a mistake.
For the sheer mountainous amount my breath it did take.
I scaled it with crampons, with rope and with guile.
As I realised the mammoth number I must file.

A plan unbidden, from dark recesses occurred.
That would mark myself out, separate from the herd.
To finish this task in record time without tire.
I would set the whole bloody lot upon fire.

With aplomb and with matches I set to make waste.
To the incredible pile but alas in my haste,
I dropped a flaming missive, ablaze in the night.
I unwittingly set the whole office alight.

'Fore long the fire department, with sirens, did appear.
The activities of my night, my guilt was quite clear.
"You did this deed, this terrible crime."
Said the judge, at my trial, sentenced four years of my time.

Fear not, for this tale, unhappy is not.
For now I'm content, happy with my lot.
A company I run, no peon am I.
Office clearances I offer, with profits sky-high.

Unconventional Tour

On the first day London Eye
If the weather is fine.
And then a stabbing in Tottenham.
See the ravens in Tower Hill
Followed by an open bus to
Peckham
Where the body still lies fresh
As the fruit at Covent Garden Market.

A mugging in New Cross
Before a show in the West End;
Probably a musical.
If it doesn't rain
A picnic in Hyde Park
Or Greenwich if you prefer
Taking in a shooting on the way,
Stopping for a bite to eat at Burger King.

The National, Tate Modern,
A drug-fuelled robbery,
And then Tate Britain; that will be a tiring day.
So have the evening off (to relax)
Because it's an early start the next day
For a double-murder in Clapham,
Where there is also a nice common.

On the final day
We have a booking for the assault
And attempted rape of a student
So don't be late.
Camden for some souvenirs
And if there is time,
Another stabbing,
Or two.
A flying visit to Buckingham Palace
And Westminster by night.
A bite to eat and an early fight
The next morning.

It's Only a Game!

The winter of '63 was renowned for the ice and the snow

But for me, it was something else that had an impact you know

For my father took me to my first football match at Burnden Park

Little did I know that this would leave such a mark.

It's easy to forget, that the only match seen live in '63

Was the FA Cup Final on an old black & white TV

So going to a match was a big event and very exciting

It was years before you would see the sight of football fans fighting

At the age of 6, I didn't know how many divisions there were

But my father told me that we were in the top one, which seemed only fair

There were no goals in the game against Leicester City but that was mainly thanks

To their goalkeeper, who pulled off save after save, his name was Gordon Banks

Unknown to me then, dark clouds were on the horizon

The player's maximum wage that had previously been frozen

Was removed, thanks to someone called Hill

And the city clubs now had their hands on the till

The town clubs couldn't survive without selling their treasure
So off went the players to give the big clubs their pleasure
We were relegated to the second tier for the first time in
thirty years
Being so young I didn't appreciate most supporters' fears.

We missed out on promotion by 6 points at our first attempt
It was the closest we came until the Greaves team of '78
We struggled to maintain our position in division two
Until in the '70-'71 season, the trap door opened and we fell
through.

The club had never been as low as this in its history
But we had a good manager and a developing youth policy
It took us only 2 years to climb back again
The future looked bright and we felt it was only a matter of
when.

But then came a shock, as our manager was tempted by
Leeds
Clough's 44 days was up and Armfield was the man to plant
new seeds
It was left to Ian Greaves, who was Armfield's assistant at the
time,
We felt confident that he would do just fine.
He had taken Huddersfield to division one not long before

With a style that was pleasing on the eye and never a bore
It took him three seasons but he got us to the Promised Land
We secured promotion at Blackburn, 20,000 of us on hand

We celebrated into the night, not worrying about our lot
Just enjoying the fact that we would give it our best shot
Unfortunately it wasn't to last, we were relegated after two
years
Bottom of the league, Greaves sacked and a return of the
tears
From there we spiralled down and down, division three and
then division four
The club was on the verge of bankruptcy, saved by a
supermarket store

Part of the ground was sold to keep the club alive
Promotion was required though, to make sure we could
survive
It came in '88 under the guidance of Phil Neal
But seven years on, we hadn't progressed a great deal
Then came a turning point, Neal was replaced by a double
act
In came Rioch and Todd, who had an immediate impact
We won promotion in their first season and went on cup
runs like never before
It was like the good old times to hear the Burnden Roar

15 years after we had last played in the top flight
We arrived there again; it was called the Premiership this time
Unfortunately Bruce was tempted by the Arsenal and left in the summer
We thanked him for 3 years of glory but it really was a bummer

We left our famous Burnden Park, in a record breaking year
It was so sad for us all but was also very clear
That we couldn't compete with the big boys with their fancy all-seater stands
With a ground that was falling to bits and not enough room for its fans

The move to the Reebok was welcomed by one and all
With its shiny new seats, corporate boxes, too many to recall
But we all reminisced of our times at Burnden Park
Where the opposition feared us, as our bite was bigger than our bark

Relegation followed by promotion followed by relegation meant
We became known as a yo-yo club, with not enough money spent
Then along came an ex, Allardyce is his name
He played for us in the '70s, a big centre half with a tendency to maim

He brought with him a revolutionary outlook on the game
Promotion came again but this time we would remain
Helped by World Cup winners, players full of flair
We bathed in the glory after all the despair

We celebrated in achieving a place in Europe twice
Playing the likes of Bayern, Athletico and Sporting under
their shining lights
Sam had done enough and went on to pastures new
We thanked him for the journey and will always be grateful
to you

We've only just survived in the last 3 seasons since Sam left
The managers we've had had left us close to death
But now we have a cracker, his name is Owen Coyle
Another old boy who will bring us to the boil

And for me, nearly fifty years on from that nil–nil draw
I've enjoyed every minute and wouldn't have changed
anything I saw
My son has followed in my footsteps and watched his first
game at the age of five
Fourteen years on, he has enjoyed being a Bolton fan for the
majority of his life

Seasons

The fading sound of the cricket bat;
Shouts of 'run' and 'how-was-that!'
The cries of the summer heat and flies
The Pimms and cider; the burger and fries

The daring thrill of shirt sleeves and shorts.
The car roof down; the weather reports.
It was fun at first, as summer awakens,
But now it grates, this summer vacation.

For they start out in brand new shades
Bearing names of half famous trades
Our gladiators, brave and true
For football is reborn anew

Summer was a fearful lapse
DIY just filling in the gaps
Literally. Till order was restored
And Saturday centres round the results Board

Did we win, did we score
Matters, but what matters more
Is the process, the thrill
Of footy, the bitter-sweet pill.

So it will run till May or more
To the unbelieving a total bore
But to those of us onside and on-board
The natural order of life is

Mondays

Mondays came around too soon,
The hassle haggle delight and groans,
The pressures on to keep them happy,
To get them in the house this Friday.

Title enquiries, searches, surveys
Drainage issues and public highways.
A lengthy talk about the fee;
Contracts exchanged to set me free.

Saturday morning arrives at last
In the car and down the coast
Coats, hats, umbrellas too,
A warming drink to induce the mood.

The whistle blows and away we go
Eighty minutes of tension unfold,
Rucks, scrums and wayward passes
Wiping the rain from my glasses.

The boys conspire to surprise us all
Winning ground and keeping ball
Opposition rallies are abated
Others thought we'd be relegated.

Five tries and it come to close
Arms aloft are my heroes
In the clubhouse debate and banter
Mondays stress doesn't really matter.

Personal

Wonder

I wake to hear your breathing rise and fall.

Curious to know of your adventures,

Wondering if, like me, sleep has brought you to another world, another time

Inhabited by faces of the past… loves, lives, dreams, fears.

Your brow furrows; worry cloaks your face

I move to pull you from your troubled slumber

Your mind and body shift bringing you to a warmer place

I hope to be the reason for the change

But realize that I will never truly know.

An Evening Love Song

I searched for beauty in the night
Hidden far from daytime's brutal light
For skies of stars and night time strolls
Through quiet beaches and star kissed shoals
Through moon-washed fields I searched alone
As a refugee searching for home
Knowing that where I stand is land
That is barren, sterile: too bland
To live, I searched to keep alive
A dream I had that love can thrive
In a world as ugly as this
Where people tell lies as they kiss
With lips too soft to make a mark
I call for beauty in the dark
To hide this truth that light uncovers
And leave just darkness for the lovers!

Waiting

Waiting… what a strange state this is.
Neither being nor not being,
Sometimes with faith, but often in fear,
Waiting for an age to pass and for thoughts to clear.

Seconds to minutes to hours and years.
A lifetime and possibly beyond;
For what if death is not the end?
Overwhelming sadness for all eternity?

Waiting for something to happen, or happen not
Moments or eons to reflect
On why and when,
Or who and what?

While eyes regard and fingers drum,
My mind unceasingly wonders what may come.
Waiting like a lonely seed,
For the light, the warmth, the food I need,
So that I may grow and bloom and… live.

For waiting is not living;
It is simply existing.
A kind of Limbo,
Dark, cold Purgatory.

Can I change the final score?
Or dare I dream of something more.
For my heart and soul are breaking, as passes the time.
Waiting, desiring, endlessly.
Will she be mine?

So, can it ever come to be?
That waiting ends.
And she
LOVES
Me

To Mum

And we look back
To our youth, with tears
Remember friends and places
Times spent;
Opportunities gone.

Should we tell our children?

And did you look back
To your youth with tears
Remembering friends and places
War times spent
Lives gone?

Did you tell your children?

Will Miriam, Peter and Nick look back
To their youth
Remember their friends, these places
Times spent with us
When we're gone?

And will they tell their children?

In the Winter

In the winter dull and dark
You don't really want to start

I don't want to prune the rose
I just want to stay here cosy

Don't ask me to go a walk
I'd much rather stay and talk

Curled up nice in my warm bed
I'm becoming a sleepy-head

Modern Life

Modern life, happy and sad, we go through it all.
Growing up happens, it makes us stand tall.
Through good times and bad, we can still feel small.
Education. Employment. Money and Debt
Like love, sex and marriage,
We take what we get.

Terminal Care (Flight's on Time)

You go there quietly, everything planned;
All angles covered by your own hand.
Decisions, revisions, what's a man to do?
Passport, ticket, it's up to you.

Your time full of memories, joys of the living;
The beauty of life, the taking: the giving.
Now with your final goal you strive,
You will conquer the Devil; he won't survive.

Us mere mortals; we are not ready to brook.
The difficult decisions you undertook,
For us it means snow, ski and fun;
You being comfortable, your race almost run.

"Have you packed this bag yourself?" she smiles,
"Enjoy your trip, Sir," see you in a while.
As the blood stops pumping on your last journey
Above your Matterhorn you are now set free.

Plans

He drives hard into the impacted days,
Forging forward to the goal
But chiselled time remained
An elusive dream.

Time fought back against the plans,
Slowed him down,
Shrouded him with its obstacles.
And all that remained,
Was himself.

It was all that he ever was
And all he ever could have been.
Events and time drifted by
And he grew older and older still

No understanding came,
No insights arose.
But instead of planning
He watches events unfold.

Curtain Call

Voices soften then quiet;
Breathing deeply, reaching within I steady,
Trying to ignite a flame;
Calling my part: struggling to muster the energy
The daily bell tolls… the curtain call

Moments pass, centre stage running through scenes,
played over and over.
Almost the bystander... observing: routine; actions;
faceless voices.

White and black fades to welcome grey.
Voices fade to silence, once again awaiting the curtain call.

The Church Bell

The church bell chimes as it
Always chimes with great precision
Marking the passing of each hour
Be it during the day or during the night
Be it winter or summer

The sweet measured sound of each ring
Dulls the pain and hurt
That each day living in a city can bring
As the sounds rest in the deepest
Recesses of my mind

The sound of each toll
Sets off an expectation – will
There be another ring, is this it?
Having woken me from my soft slumber
And induced me to listen for longer
Will you like a seductress
Fade away slowly into the inky night
Leaving me to wonder, if only?

Your sonorous sound becomes entwined
In so many different memories – the
Peal of joyous sound as a young
Couple newly married emerge from a church
Your sombre heavy sound as a
Coffin emerges from a church
Your rapturous sound as proud parents
Emerge from a church holding
Their newly anointed baby
Each of your strikes announces
Love, happiness and pain in
Equal disinterested measure

Will your sound haunt me, caress me,
Love me or hurt me; or

Will the proclamation of your sound be
As I have always known it to be –
Both the harbinger of a darkness yet to fall
And the sound that heralds a hope and
A new future for us all.

The 21st Century Brother

My brother smokes. Why, oh why, does my brother smoke?
Was it because my parents smoked?
Did he think it was cool?
Was it because would find him hot?
Well it's not hot! It's not cool! He is a fool.
WHY? WHY? WHY?

He has Asthma, his lungs are black and his health is crap.
He thinks he's invincible.
He says it helps him relax but I can see his time running out.
WHY? WHY? WHY?

He looks so pale and sallow.
His fingers are stained yellow.
He smells like a bin and tastes of dog ends.
WHY? WHY? WHY?

And what if he could no longer smoke his death sticks?
Would he breakdown, shakedown or look like a twit?
No. He would live longer, be stronger and more prosperous.
WHY? WHY? WHY?

Your Sister

Such a Muddle

The dread of facing yet another day
Why did I want to run away?
At the time it seemed a good idea
But with it always came one big fear
Who would look after my two boys?
And clear up all their many toys.

Middle Age

Earlier this year my Granddad died.
At his funeral we laughed and cried,
We tried to hide our feelings, keep them inside
But I just felt full of pride
That I knew him

It was truly a great day,
Not the fact he's now gone away, of course
But it was his last chance to say, to all of us there that day
You are family, don't be strangers how ever far you may
stray
Keep close

When I was a boy, we would always spend
Time with my uncle John, each weekend at his home
He lived alone, we were his family and he was my friend
And when I was 12 I thought this would never end
But of course, it did.

And standing there that day back in March
Wrapped up warm against the harsh winds it dawned on
me
In the garden of remembrance near the oak tree
As I looked across at my uncle John
It's been 30 years

He looked now, like my Granddad did when I was 12
And I guess I look like he did then.
Time takes its toll on all men, and again a realisation
How long is life
And how we waste it

I am now what they call Middle Aged.
My son is 12 and it seems so strange
That time will play such a cruel game
And finally I will become the same
As my uncle John and my Granddad

Time cannot be stopped and nor should we
Attempt to work against it or worry
About the things we can't control, but does it mean
That I am halfway through my life, it seems so
Sometimes I hope not

Hang the Consequences

My favourite colour is grey
"He's such a dullard," people say
I don't let my own views get in the way
So never ask me for an opinion.
I've found my best defence
Is make sure I'm sitting on the fence
And so I never take a chance
So don't ask me for an opinion

My wife's the one who buys
My stripy shirts and ties
So I will never be surprised
By the changing face of fashion
I know she is always right
And that's why we never fight
We make love each Sunday night
But it's never filled with passion

My desires have all been killed
By the persona I have built
A life so unfulfilled
But even dullards still have dreams
My existence is a mistake
Not a ripple shall I make
No one to follow in my wake
But my life's not as it seems

The history books have shown
That one must sail one's ship alone
And have opinions of one's own
So I'm done sitting on fences
To justify my life
I'm going out to buy a knife
Then I'm going to kill my wife
And hang the consequences

Observations

Out of my darkness	–	Light
Out of my sadness	–	Happiness
Out of my despair	–	Hope
Out of my emptiness	–	Love

Poet Biographies

The poets who contributed their verses to this volume are all professionals working in companies and organisations that are often exposed to public scrutiny. For this reason, almost all the *Poetry for Now* contributors requested that their work should be published anonymously.

However, each contributor has agreed to provide a brief biography, designed to help the reader put these verses into context by giving an indication of their profession and hobbies. These are printed below and we hope that they will provide a glimpse of the diverse range of people and personalities whose work is included here.

An equity trader at an investment bank whose hobbies include swimming, rock music and West Ham United:

A specialist tax advisor whose hobbies include walking, travel, restaurants and collecting old films:

A financial planning consultant whose hobbies include hill walking, fishing and collecting whisky:

A financial funds manager whose hobbies include travel, history
books and cooking:

A chartered account whose hobbies include gardening, golf, family
and rugby:

A barrister whose hobbies include the theatre, writing and
philosophy:

A specialist financial adviser whose hobbies include skiing, world
travel, movies and listening to music:

An investment banker whose hobbies include golf, reading and
music:

A financial consultant whose hobbies include Gaelic football, the Irish
language and travelling:

A doctor specialising in bowel cancer whose hobbies include skiing,
music and running:

A GP in a rural practice whose hobbies include gardening, bee keeping and rugby:

A family GP whose hobbies include music, reading and family:

A company director whose hobbies include skiing, movies and travel:

A hospital doctor whose hobbies include sport and movies:

A director of a pharmacy whose hobbies include sailing, snowboarding and motorbikes:

A professional writer whose hobbies include current affairs, tennis and politics:

A dental surgeon whose hobbies include playing football, travelling, film and music:

A commercial director whose hobbies include skiing, salmon fishing and running:

And so concludes *Poetry for Now*.

Think YOU can do better?

Why not leave a comment at

www.poetryfornow.com

or even submit something of your own!

Lightning Source UK Ltd.
Milton Keynes UK
UKOW030253050213

205821UK00001B/2/P